Madge and the Beanstalk

Written by Alison Hawes

Illustrated by Kevin McAleenan

Madge put some magic beans in the soil, and a gigantic beanstalk grew in her garden.

One day, Madge said, "I'm going to
go to the top of my magic beanstalk."

It took all of Madge's energy, but she did manage to get to the top.

She could see a large palace.
"It's a giant's palace!" she thought.

Madge crept up to the giant's palace.
She looked through the window.
The giant was asleep.

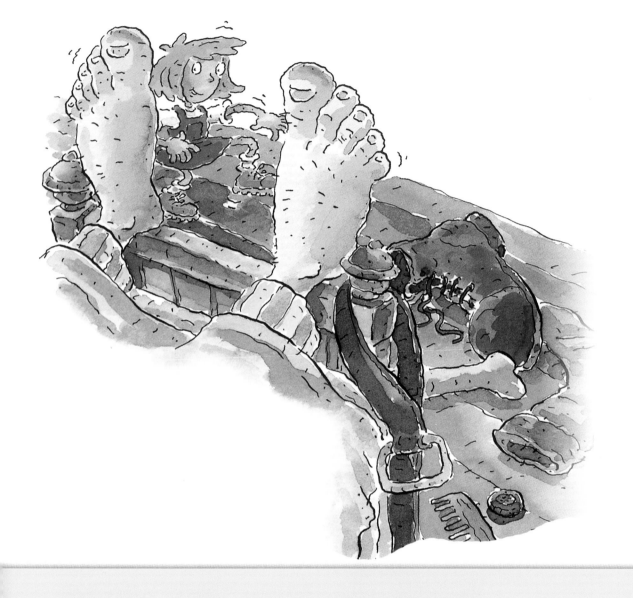

Madge crept inside the gigantic palace. "I'll just see what I can find," she said.

Madge saw a golden harp. It was a magic harp.

Then Madge saw a white hen. It was
a magic hen.

Then Madge found some large bags of gold. She lifted one up gently, so it did not make a noise. "I'm going to be rich!" she said.

But the magic hen and the magic harp called out to the giant and woke him up. "Stop!" the giant shouted at Madge.

Madge ran out of the giant's palace.
The giant was charging behind her in
a rage.
"I've got to get back home!" she cried,
running to dodge the huge hands.

She slid to the bottom of the magic
beanstalk. But the giant began to charge
down, too. It took all Madge's energy to
chop down the huge beanstalk.

The gigantic beanstalk began to twist and sway.

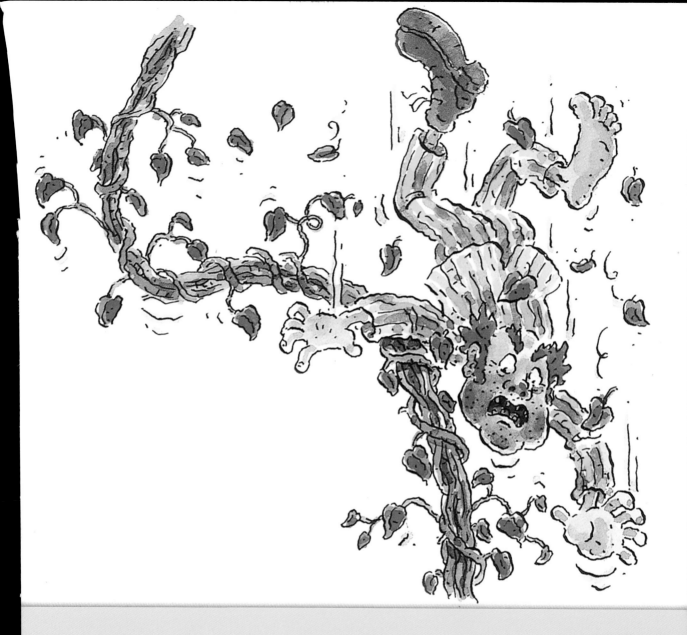

The giant could not manage to hold
on and he fell into a hedge.

Then Madge lifted the large bag of
gold, the magic hen and the magic harp
and she quickly ran into her cottage.